NERF COLORING BOOK
Color Your Blasters Collection

DEMOLISHER 2-IN-1

Nerf Gun Coloring Book Collection Series

Copyright: Published by Chawanun C. in 2018
Illustrations and design © 2018 Chawanun C.

ISBN : 978-1790202522

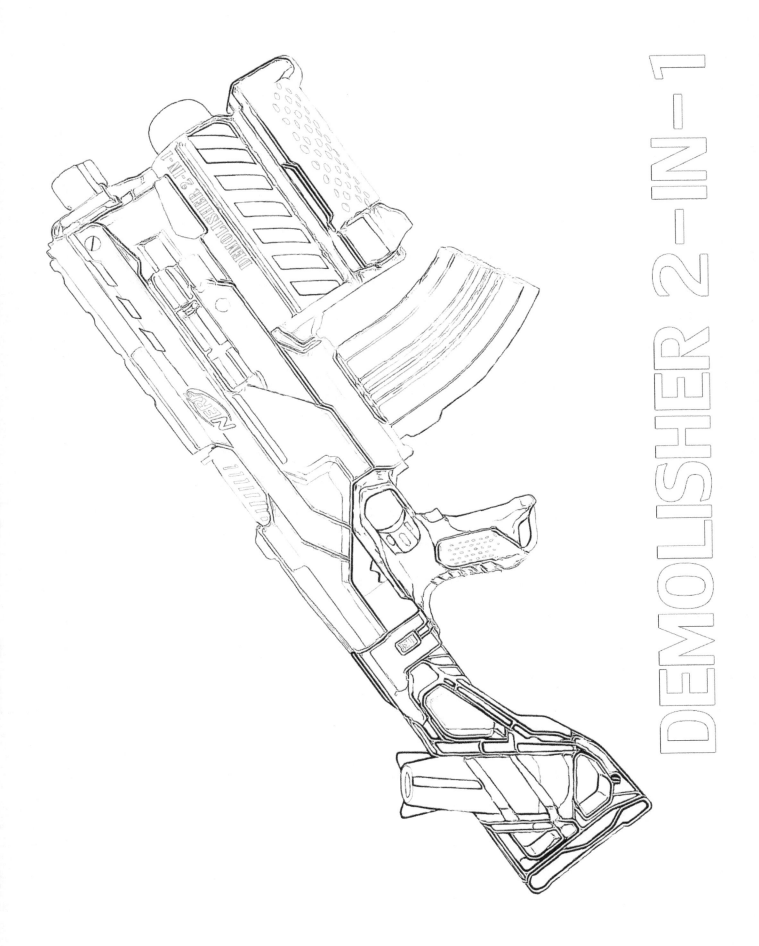

DEMOLISHER 2-IN-1

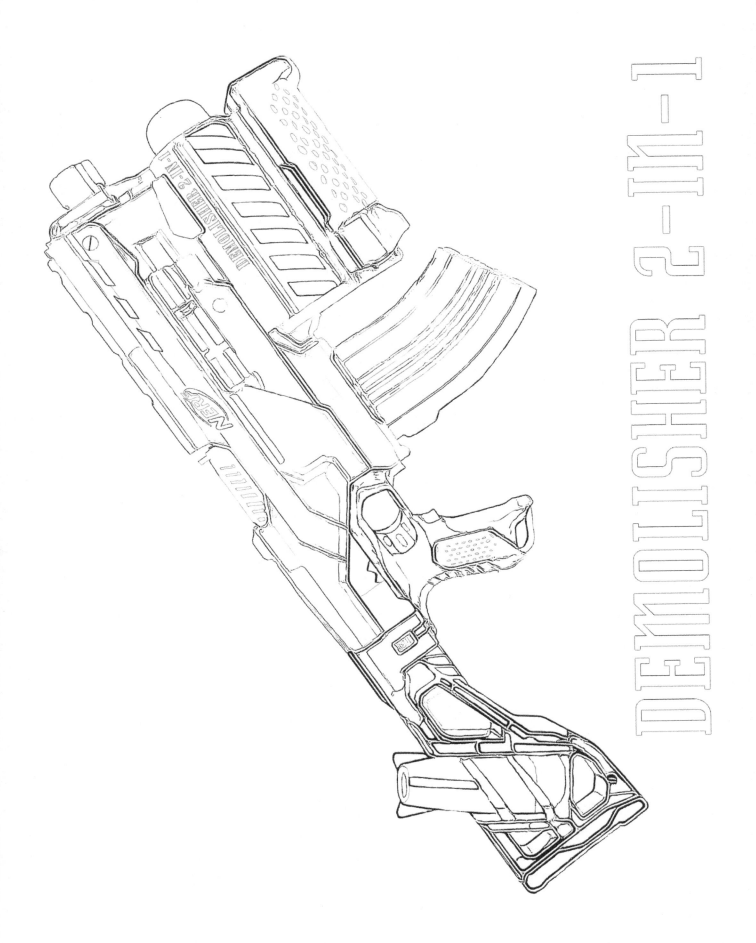

DEMOLISHER 2-IN-1

DEMOLISHER 2-IN-1

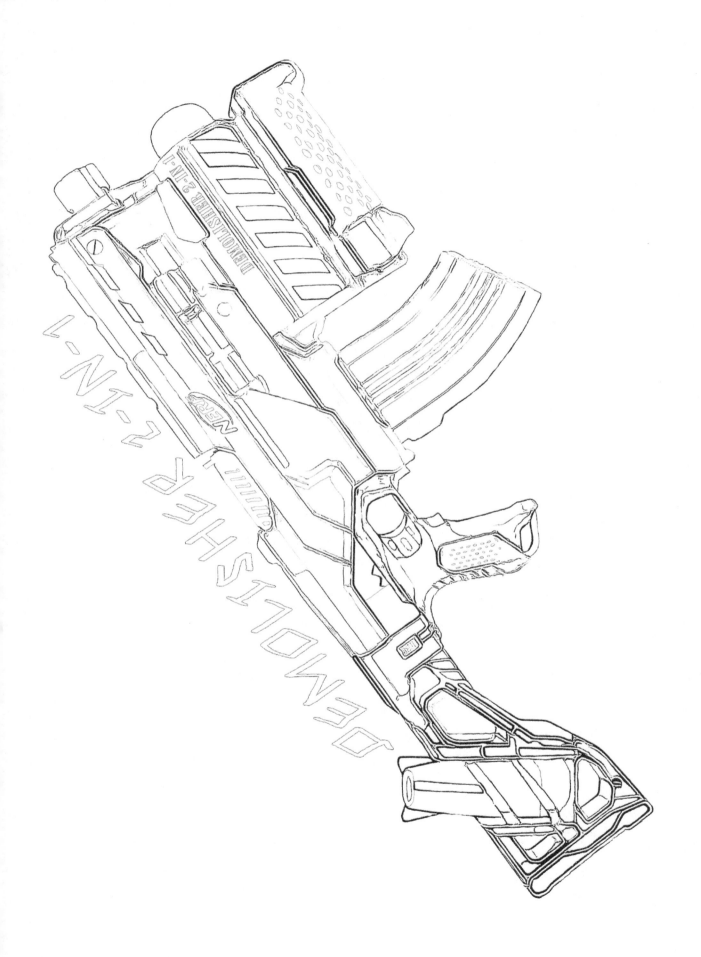

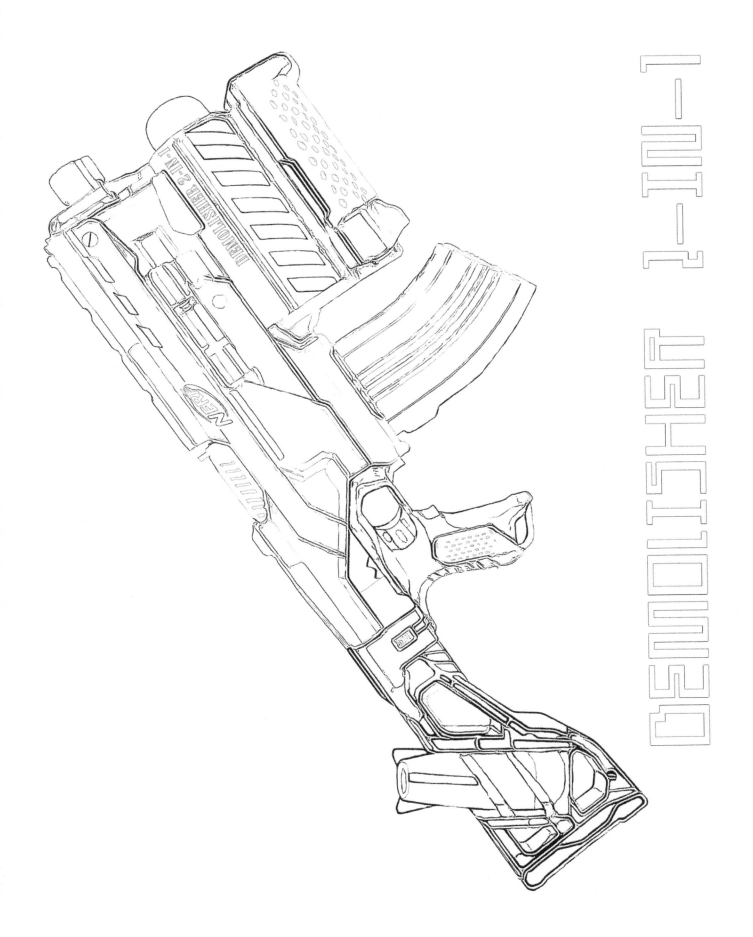

DEMOLISHER 1-IN-1

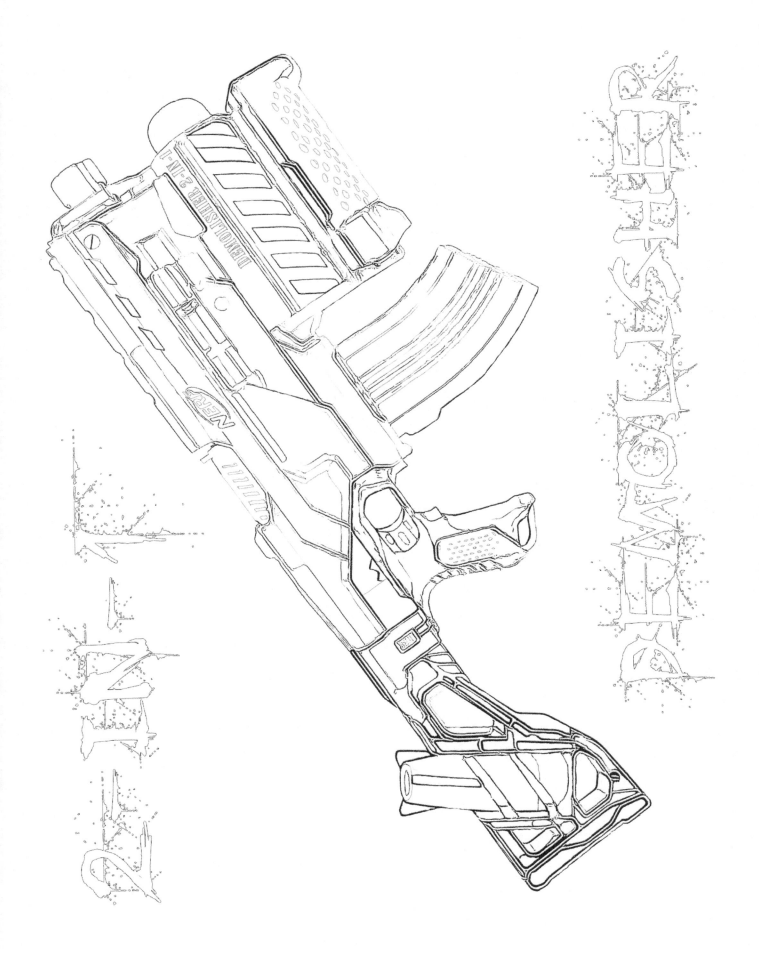

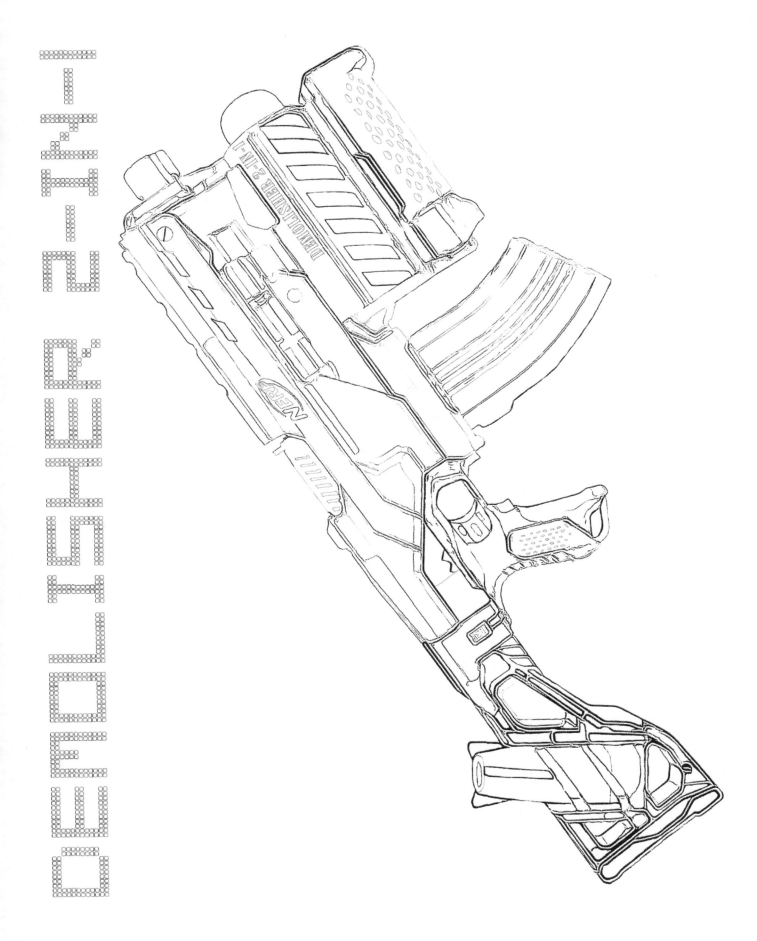

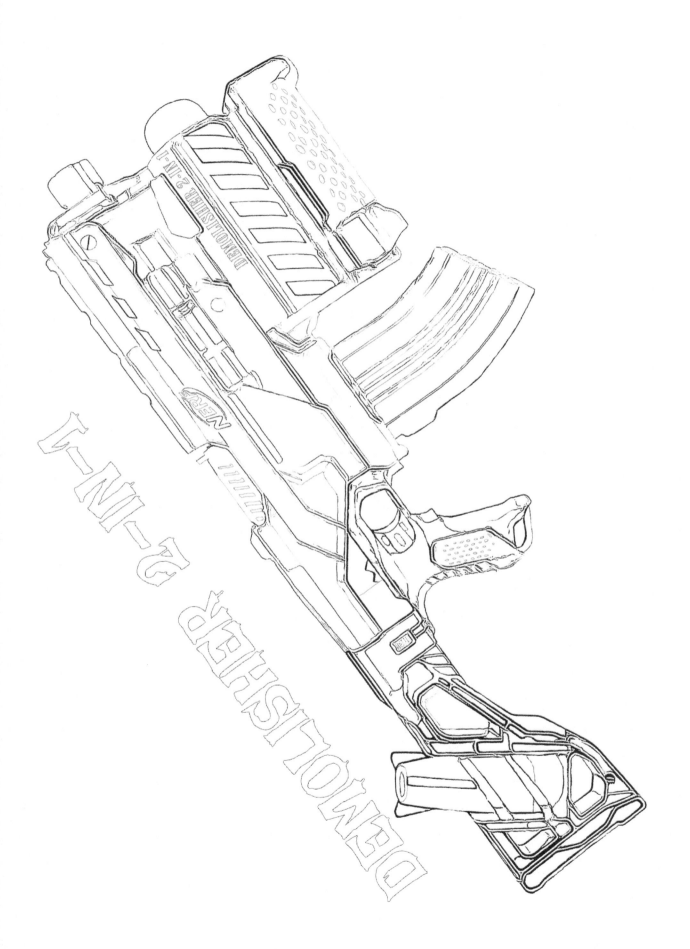

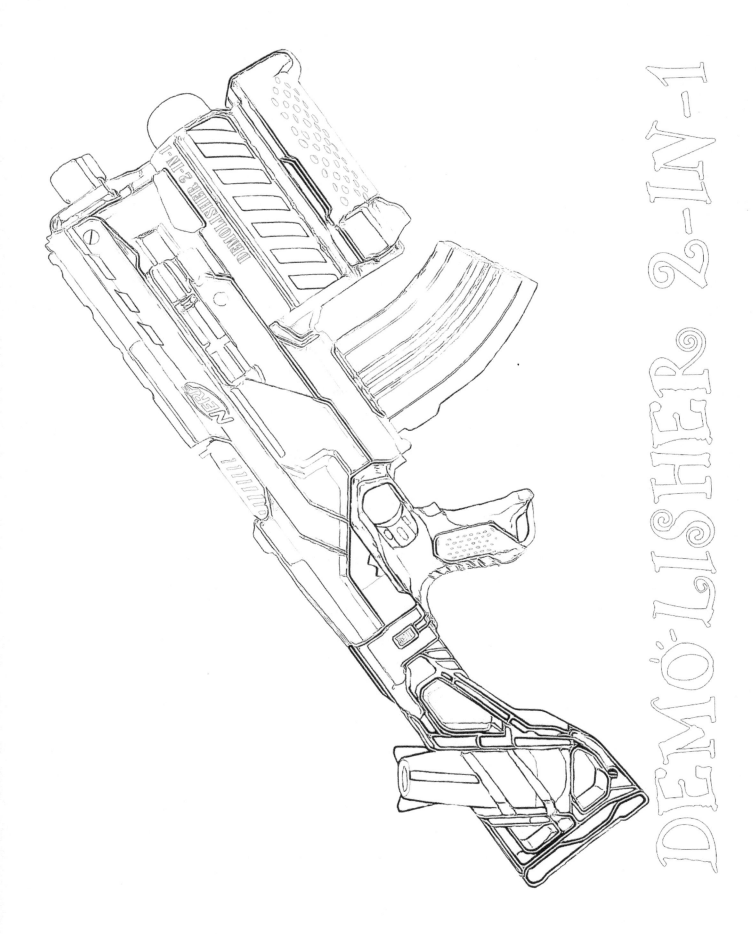

DEMO-LISHER 2-IN-1

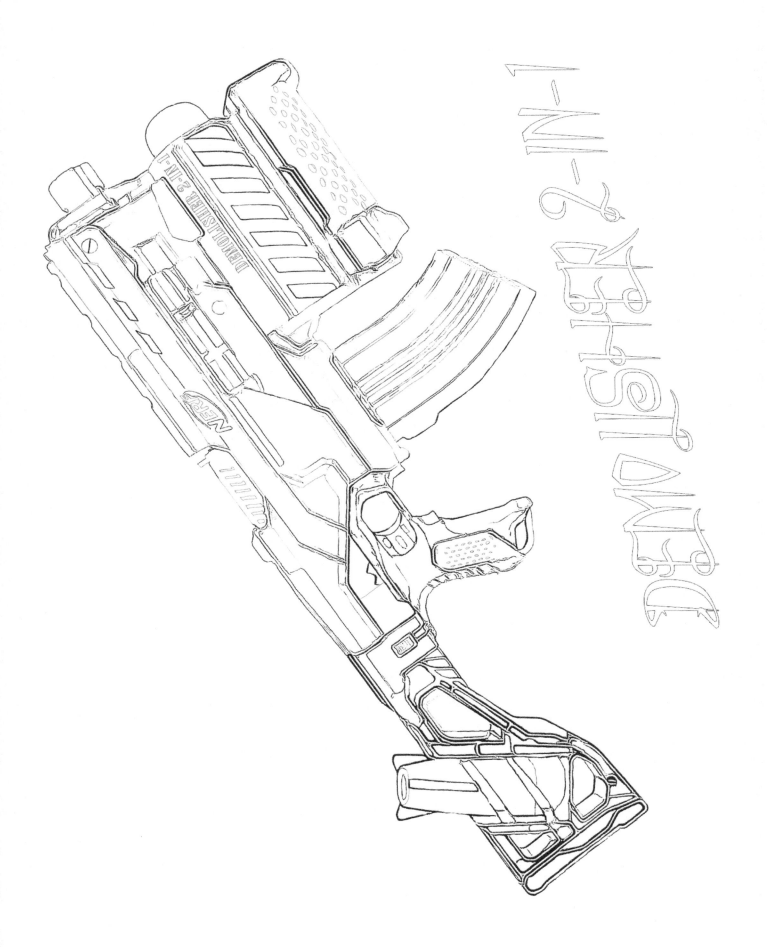

DEMOLISHER 2-IN-1

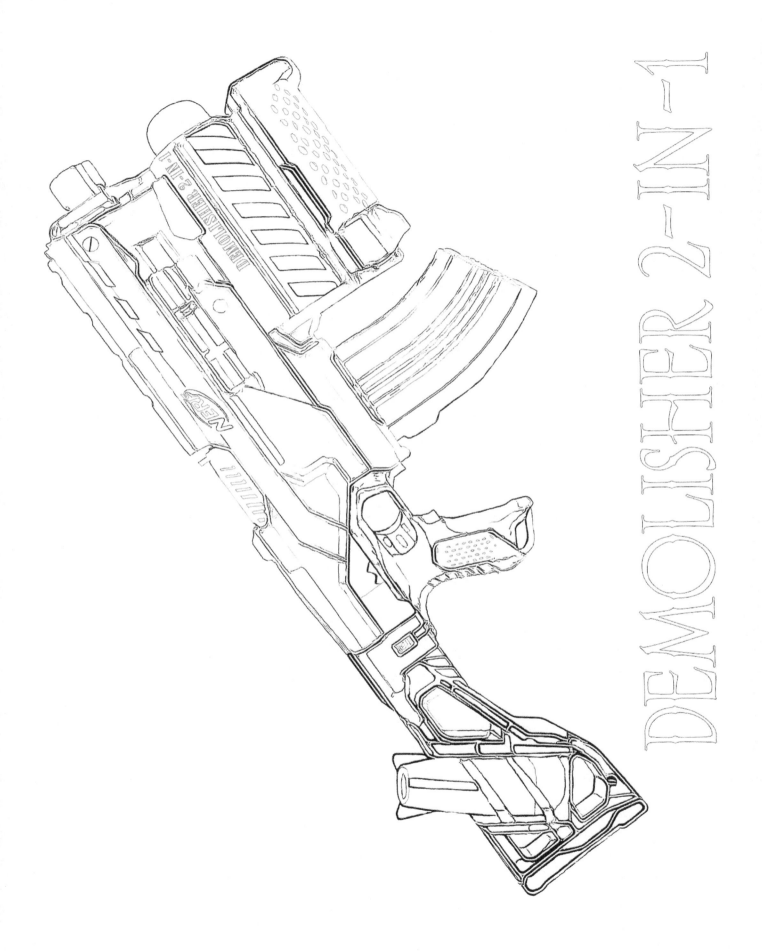

DEMOLISHER 2-IN-1

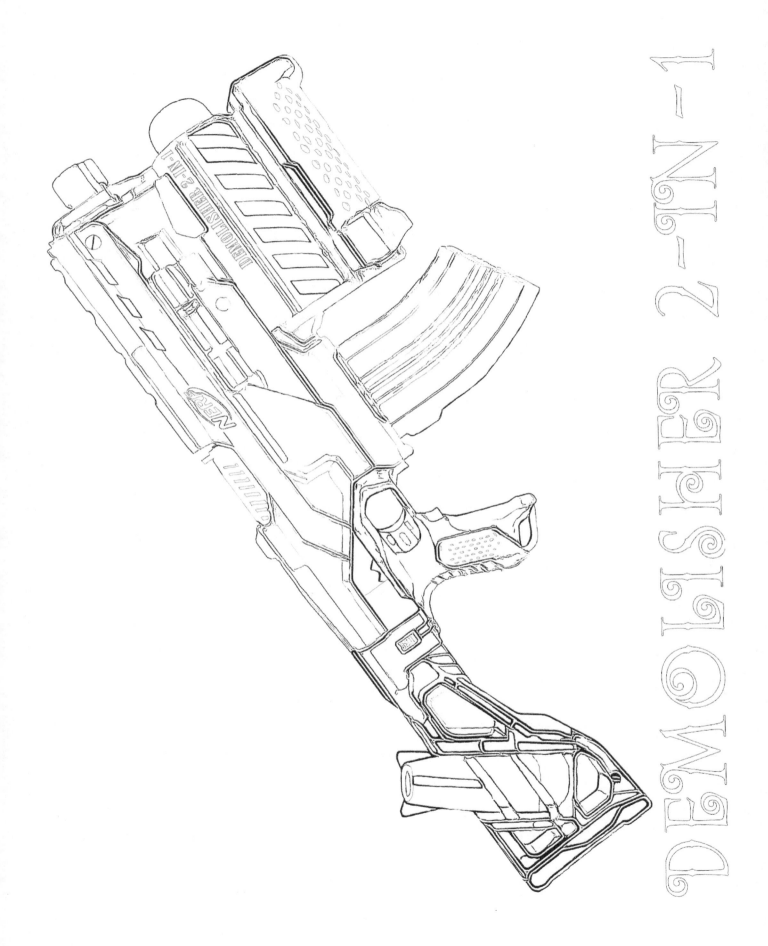

DEMOLISHER 2-IN-1

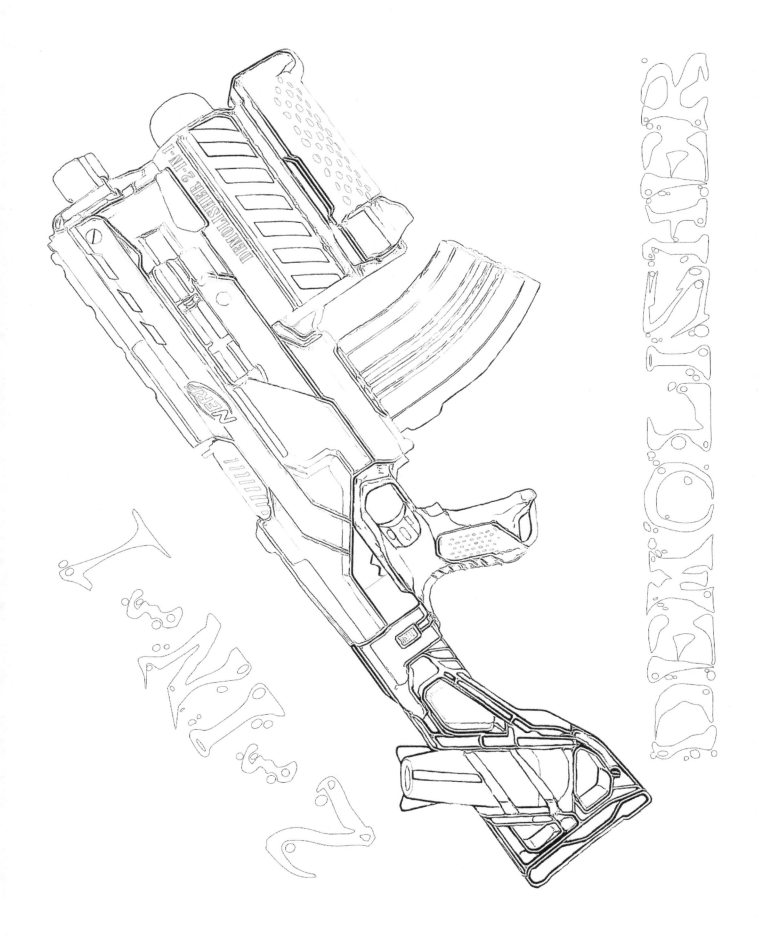

DEMOLISHER 2-IN-1

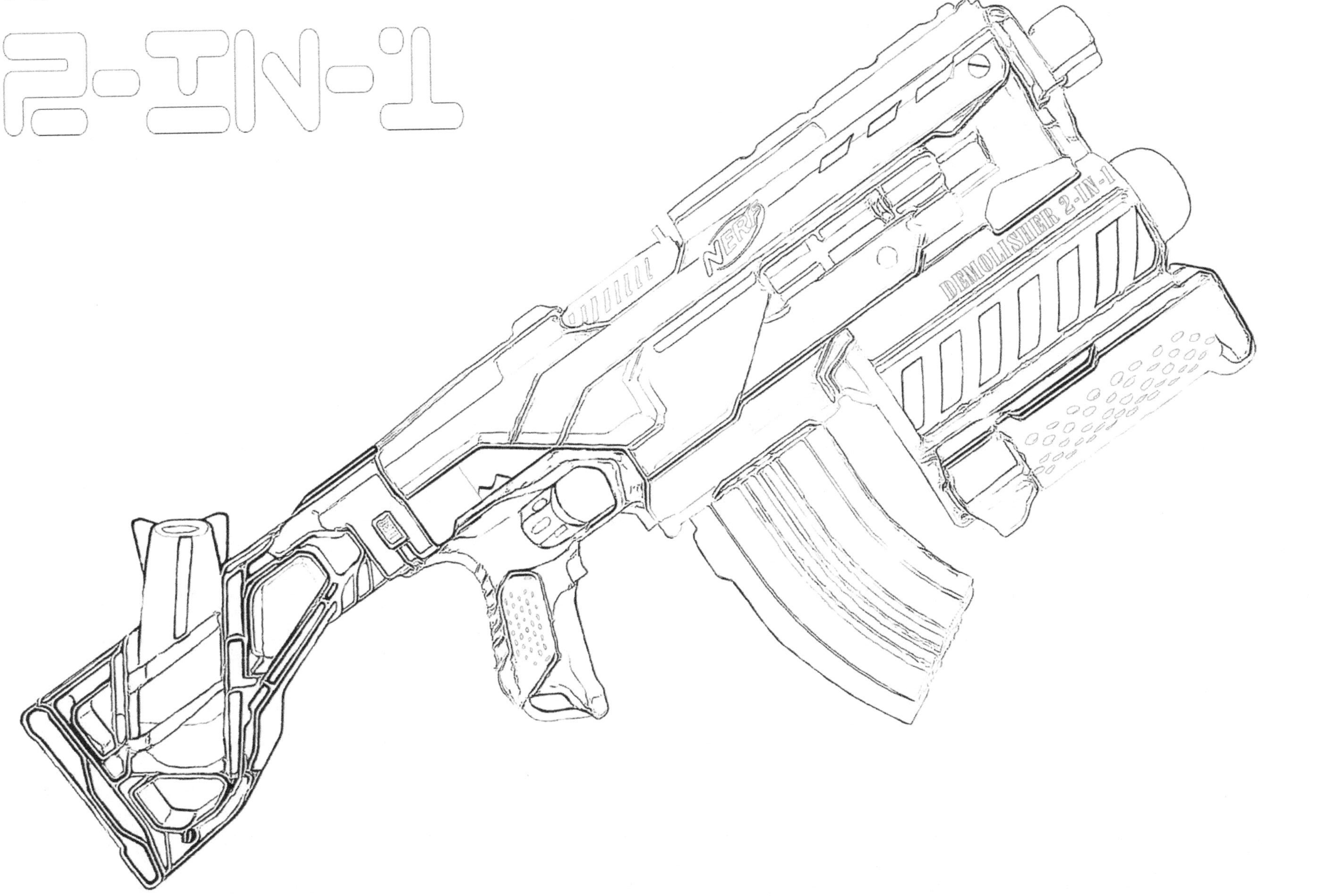

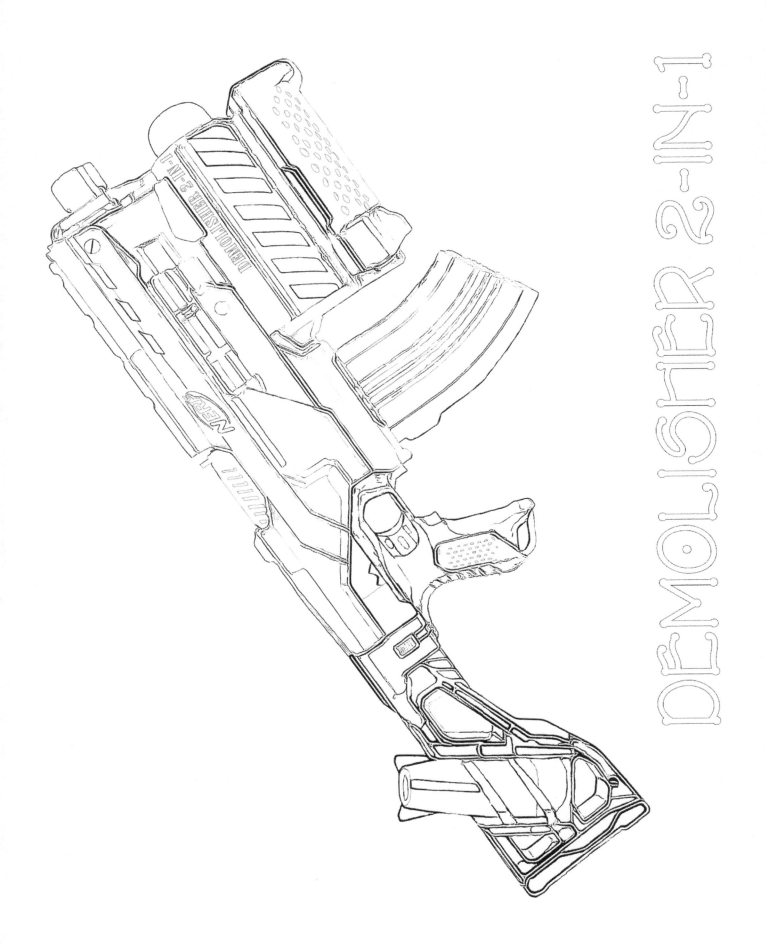

DEMOLISHER 2-IN-1

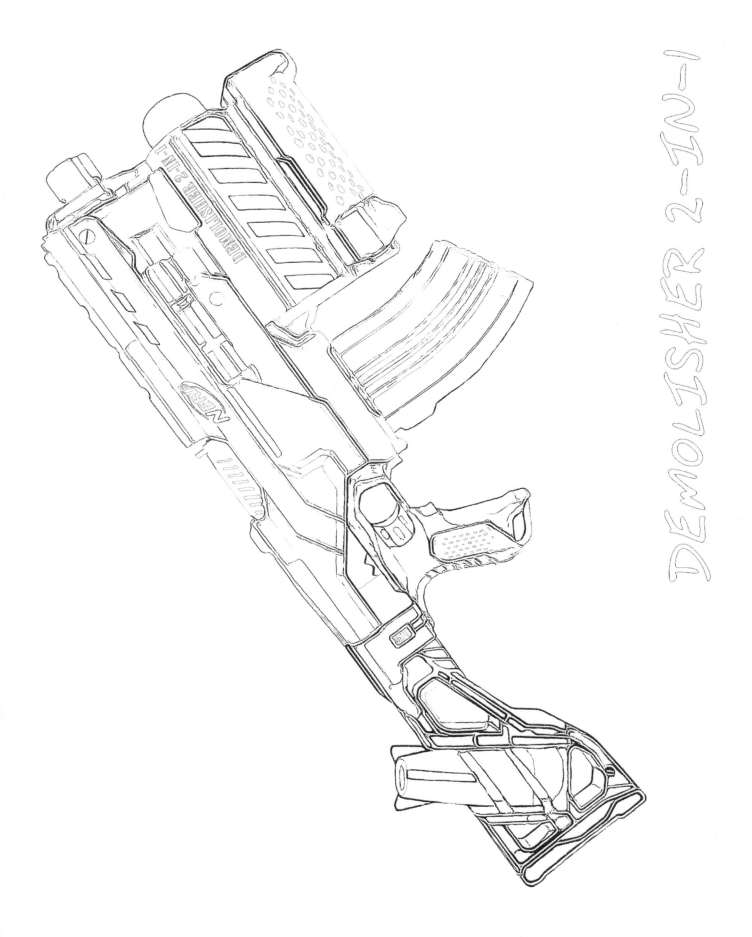

DEMOLISHER 2-IN-1

DEMOLISHER
2-IN-1

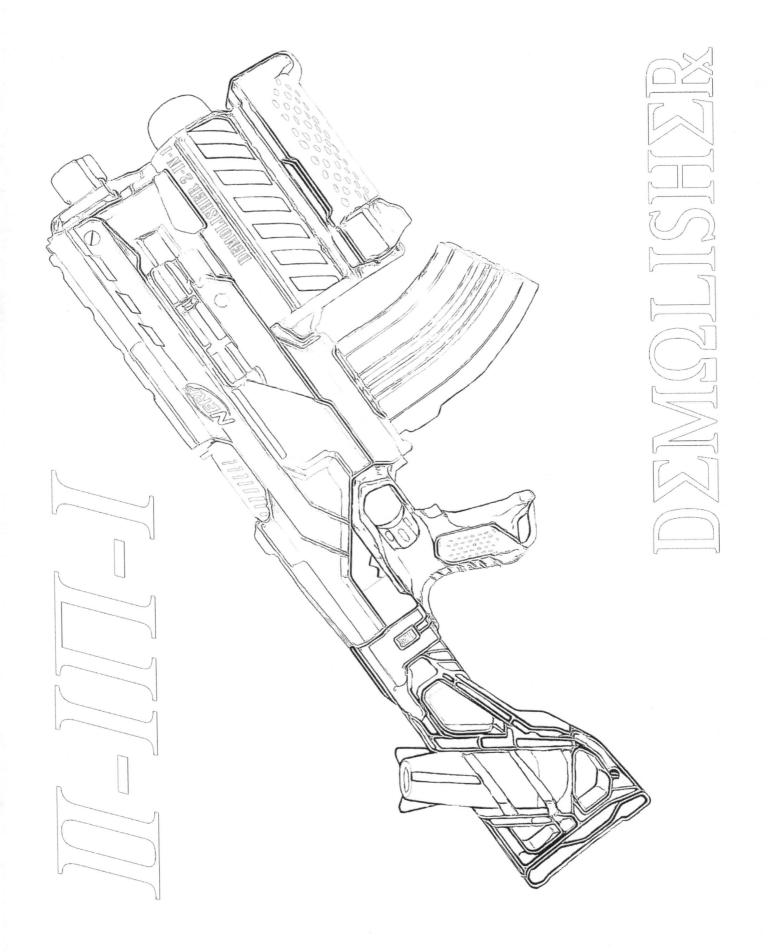

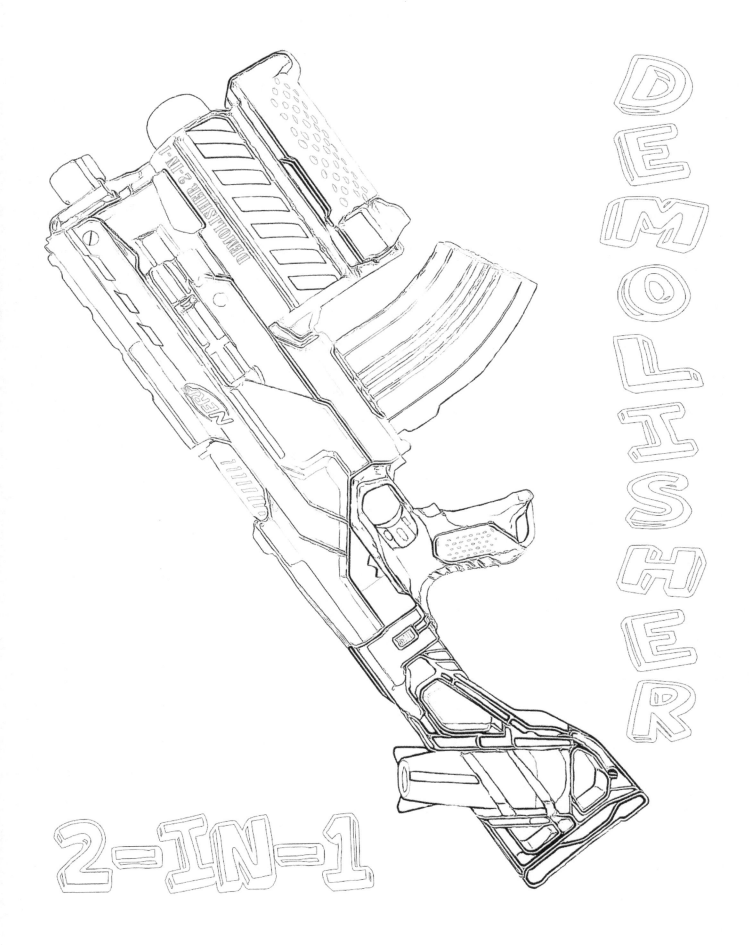

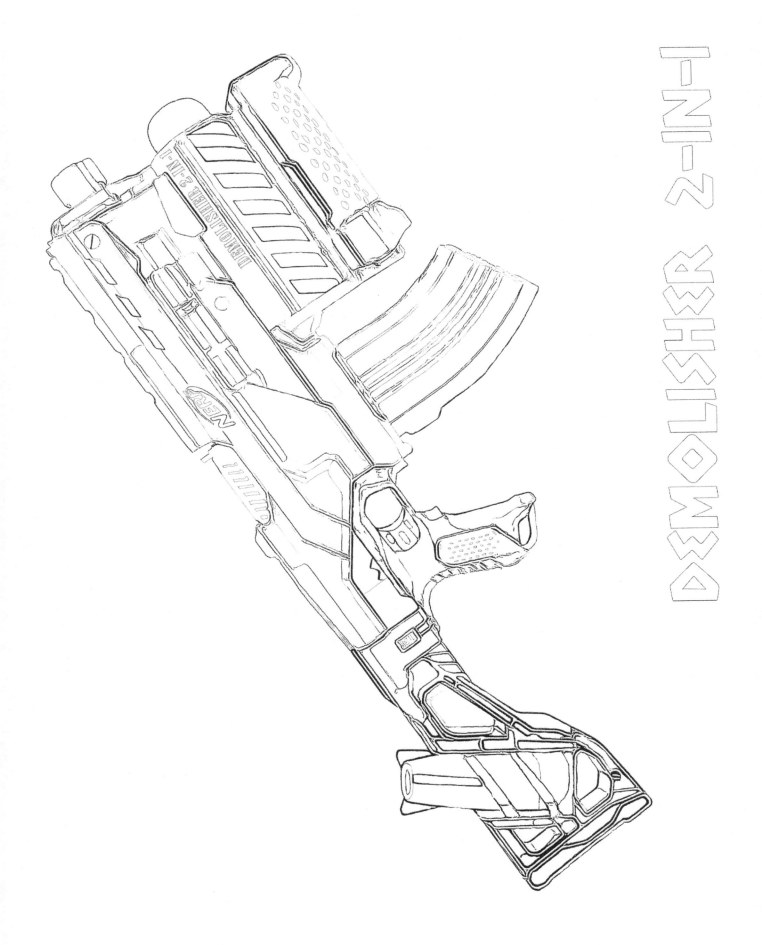

DEMOLISHER 2-IN-1

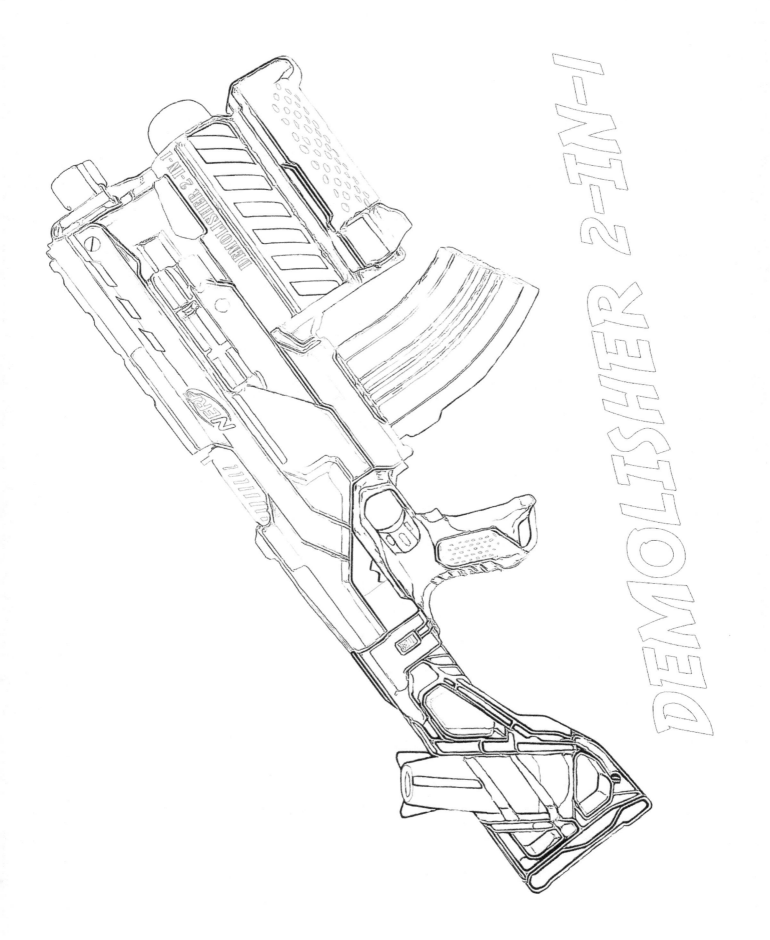

DEMOLITSHER 2-IN-1

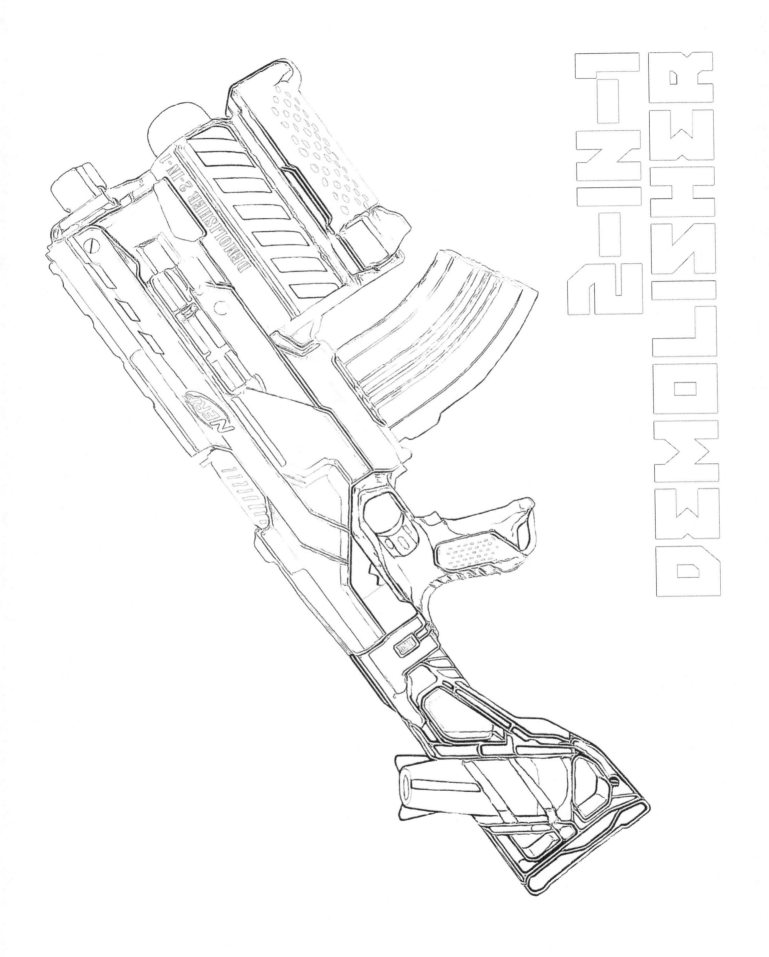

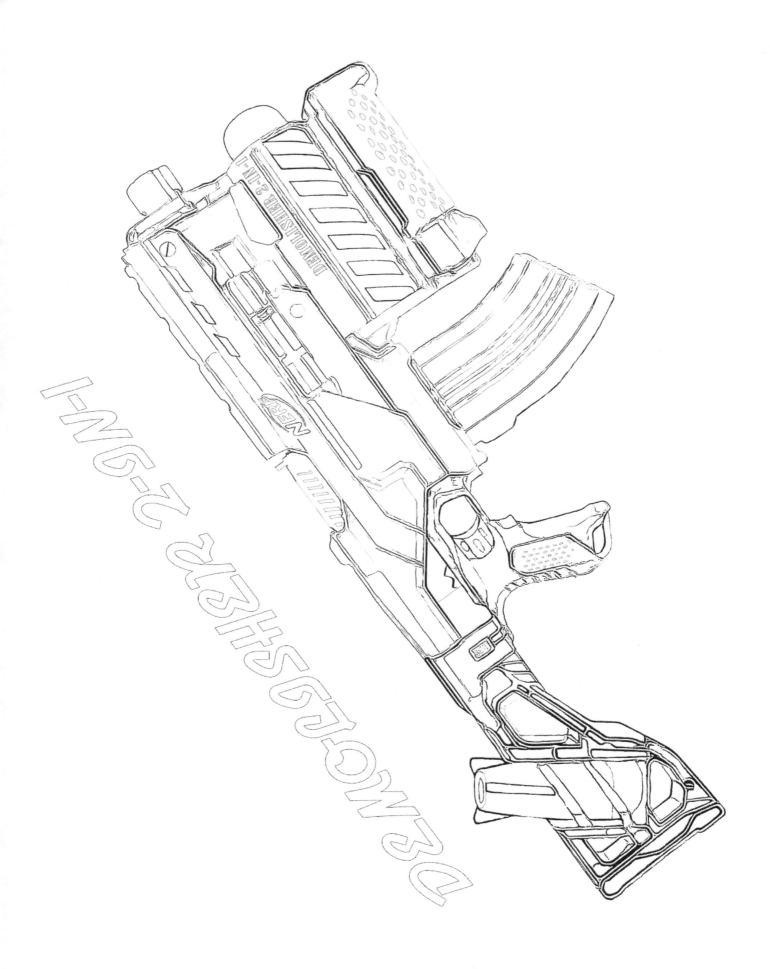

DEMOLISHER 2-IN-1

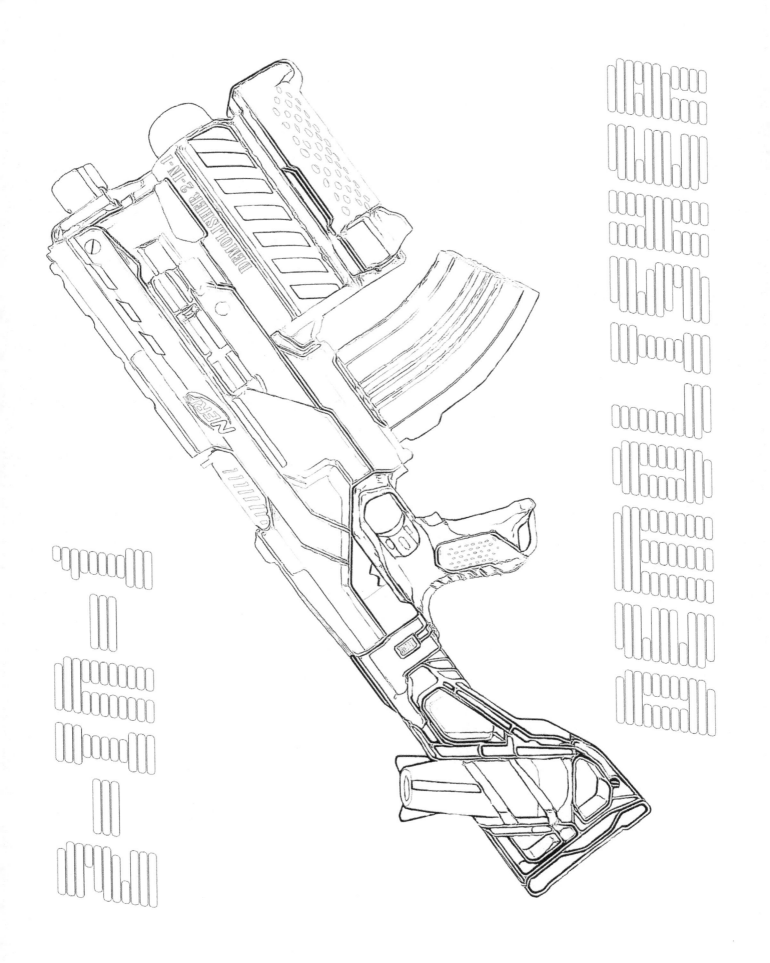

Hope you enjoy this NERF Coloring Book Collection.

Thank you.

Made in the USA
Coppell, TX
01 June 2023

17583000R00031